D1611349

TREAT THE EARTH GENTLY

TREAT THE EARTH GENTLY

The Friendship
Of Man and Nature
In Inspiring Words
And Photographs
Selected by
Beverly Simmons Bearly

♛ Hallmark Editions

PHOTOGRAPHS:
Dr. E. R. Degginger: *Dust Jacket.*
Charles Steinhacker: *Page 20, Endpapers.*
Maxine Jacobs: *Title Page, Pages 36-37.*
Larry West: *Page 4.* Sue Morey: *Pages 8-9.*
Richard Fanolio: *Page 12.* Gerard Baumgarten: *Page 17.*
Neal and Molly Jansen: *Pages 24-25.*
Dr. William J. Weber: *Pages 32, 44.*
Jim Cozad: *Pages 29, 41.*

TREAT THE EARTH GENTLY

We receive but what we give,
And in our life alone does Nature live . . . .

SAMUEL TAYLOR COLERIDGE

To be beautiful and to be calm is the
ideal of nature.

RICHARD JEFFERIES

Nature is perfect, wherever we look, but man always deforms it.

J. C. F. SCHILLER

The beaten earth appears defeated and dead, but it only appears so.

JOHN STEINBECK

The great question . . . shall we surrender to our surroundings, or shall we make peace with nature and begin to make reparations for the damage we have done to our air, our land and our water?

RICHARD M. NIXON

In the concert of nature it is hard to keep in tune with oneself if one is out of tune with everything.

GEORGE SANTAYANA

A tree is a nobler object than a prince in his coronation robes.

ALEXANDER POPE

Nothing is more beautiful than the loveliness of the woods before sunrise.

GEORGE WASHINGTON CARVER

The source of man's unhappiness is his ignorance of Nature.

PAUL HENRY THIRY D'HOLBACH

Mountains have a dreamy way
Of folding up a noisy day
In quiet covers, cool and gray.

LEIGH BUCKNER HANES

It is a curious situation that the sea,
from which life first arose, should
now be threatened by the activities
of one form of that life.

RACHEL CARSON

God bless the flowers so lovely, so
easy to die. They force us to be gentle.

JOSEPH PINTAURO

What is lovely never dies, but passes into other loveliness, stardust or sea-foam, flower or winged air.

THOMAS BAILEY ALDRICH

Man has lost the capacity to foresee and to forestall. He will end by destroying the earth.

ALBERT SCHWEITZER

Nature never breaks her own laws.

LEONARDO DA VINCI

That the sky is brighter than the earth
means little unless the earth itself is
appreciated and enjoyed.

HELEN KELLER

We have forgotten the earth, forgotten it in the sense that we fail to regard it as a source of our life.

FAIRFIELD OSBORN

The hills are going somewhere; they have been on the way a long time.

HILDA CONKLING

There is no other door to knowledge than the door nature opens; there is no truth except the truths we discover in nature.

LUTHER BURBANK

Accuse not Nature, she hath done
her part; do thou but thine.

JOHN MILTON

There is a true music of Nature:
the song of the birds,
the whisper of leaves,
the ripple of waters upon a sandy
    shore,
and the wail of wind or sea.

JOHN LUBBOCK

We have not run out of water; we
have simply run out of new streams
to pollute.

E. ROY TINNEY

The sky
is that beautiful old parchment
in which the sun and the moon
keep their diary.

ALFRED KREYMBORG

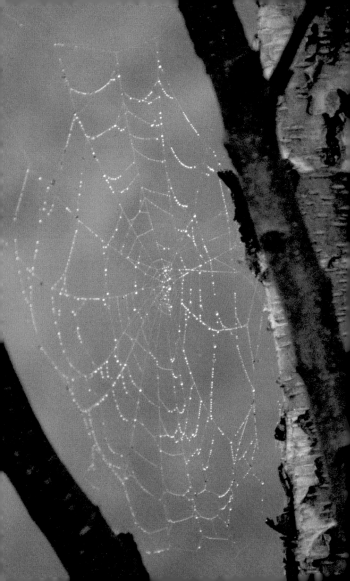

We travel together, passengers on a little spaceship, dependent on its vulnerable supplies of air and soil. . . .

ADLAI STEVENSON

Nature never deceives us; it is always we who deceive ourselves.

JEAN JACQUES ROUSSEAU

Nature is full of genius, full of the divinity, so that not a snowflake escapes its fashioning hand.

HENRY DAVID THOREAU

The sun is not yet risen,
But the dawn lies red on the dew.

SAMUEL TAYLOR COLERIDGE

The whole country suffers every time
Americans make a bad choice, even
a local one, that allows the needless
waste of any of our natural treasures.
The destruction of such resources is
irrevocable; no one can pass that way
again.

LIFE MAGAZINE EDITORIAL

Nature is often hidden, sometimes overcome, seldom extinguished.

FRANCIS BACON

The concern is not with nature alone, but with the total relation between man and the world around him. Its object is not just man's welfare but the dignity of man's spirit.

LYNDON B. JOHNSON

What place is so rugged and so homely that there is no beauty, if you only have a feeling for beauty?

HENRY WARD BEECHER

Nature is the art of God.

DANTE

I wonder nature don't retire
From public life disgusted.

W. S. GILBERT

Man's daily life and his aspirations
cannot be thought of apart from natural events because they are the ulti-
mate expressions of our living Earth.

RENE DUBOS

Laws of Nature are God's thoughts thinking themselves out in the orbits and the tides.

C. H. PARKHURST

A River is more than an Amenity—it is a Treasure.

OLIVER WENDELL HOLMES

The big problems of man's relation to his environment have resulted from his own actions.

ELVIS J. STAHR

Everything is perfect coming from the hands of the Creator; everything degenerates in the hands of man.

JEAN JACQUES ROUSSEAU

. . . to the soft grass clothing the earth
How slight is the praise we render.

EDGAR FAWCETT

Ever charming, ever new,
When will the landscape tire
   the view?

Nature is simply something indis-
pensable, like air and light and water,
that we accept as necessary to living,
and the nearer we can get to it the
happier we are.

LOUISE DICKENSON RICH

Let us permit nature to have her way: she understands her business better than we do.

MICHEL DE MONTAIGNE

Dewdrops and pollens may I enjoy. With these may it be beautiful in front of me.

NAVAJO SONG

And this, our life, exempt from public haunt, finds tongues in trees, books in the running brooks, sermons in stones, and good in everything.

WILLIAM SHAKESPEARE

Science has found that nothing disappears without a trace. Nature does not know extinction. All it knows is transformation.

WERNHER VON BRAUN

When you defile the pleasant streams
And the wild bird's abiding place,
You massacre a million dreams
And cast your spittle in God's face.

JOHN DRINKWATER

How many more generations will pass before it will have become nearly impossible to be alone even for an hour, to see anywhere nature as she is without man's improvements upon her?

JOSEPH WOOD KRUTCH

Forget not that the earth delights to feel your bare feet and the winds long to play with your hair.

KAHLIL GIBRAN

It is in this unearthly first hour of spring twilight that earth's almost agonized livingness is most felt.

ELIZABETH BOWEN

Make the earth attractive to the rest of the universe.

JOSEPH PINTAURO

The sun shines into cesspools but is not corrupted.

DIOGENES LAERTIUS

The light died in the low clouds. Falling snow drank in the dusk. Shrouded in silence, the branches wrapped me in their peace. When the boundaries were erased, once again the wonder: that I exist.

DAG HAMMARSKJÖLD

If there is magic on this planet, it is contained in water....

LOREN EISELEY

We do not see nature with our eyes, but with our understandings and our hearts.

WILLIAM HAZLITT

Like a great poet, nature produces the greatest results with the simplest means. There are simply a sun, flowers, water, and love.

HEINRICH HEINE

The sea I found
Calm as a cradled child in dreamless
    slumber bound.

P. B. SHELLEY

Our dedicated and thoughtful stewardship of this Nation's resources and environment will determine mankind's future to a far more meaningful degree than armaments and diplomacy.

JULIA BUTLER HANSEN

Science will never be able to reduce the value of a sunset to arithmetic.

LOUIS ORR

We have misused our land and allowed our wastes to pollute and destroy our air and waters. Mankind must change its ways or accept the very real prospect of extinction.

JOHN D. DINGELL

...Part of our love must be expressed by our relation to all living organisms and organic structures; some of our love must go to sea and river and soil, restraining careless exploitation and pollution . . . .

LEWIS MUMFORD

Leave it as it is. . . . The ages have been at work on it, and man can only mar it.

THEODORE ROOSEVELT

Set in Optima,
a Roman face of graceful simplicity
designed by Hermann Zapf.
Printed on Hallmark Crown Royale paper.
Designed by Beth Hedstrom.